## A MEDIUM SIZED BOOK OF
# BORING CAR TRIVIA

D1332830

Effort has been made to ensure the information in this book is accurate and honest but mistakes happen. If you're going to write in to complain, please remember to start your message with the words, "I think you'll find…"

ISBN: 9798638657918
Second edition

sniffpetrol.com

# CONTENTS

Belgium didn't have a compulsory driving test until 1977

# INTRODUCTION

For many years whenever I've heard an obscure and arcane car fact I've tried to make a note of it, usually in one of three ways. In descending order of reliability they are; on my phone, scribbled on an old receipt, and in my brain. I recorded these tiny slivers of information largely for my own amusement, and maybe so that I could impress people at parties by dispensing these facts in sentences that started, "Well, actually…" Unfortunately, I didn't get to do this since I didn't get invited to any parties, largely on account of this habit.

Recently I realised that I'd amassed so many facts, some fully formed, others shoddily half-remembered, that there was enough for some kind of compendium of barely interesting things and when I mentioned this on Twitter I was amazed at the positive response to the idea. So here we are. If you expressed vague enthusiasm on social media, this is all your fault. And thank you. This has given me something to do during The Age of Boredom.

I'm sure there are mistakes and errors in this book. I just didn't spot them. I'm equally sure you will point them out to me later and I will hang my nerdish head in shame. Until then, enjoy the boring car trivia. And try not to nod off.

Richard Porter, Sniff Petrol
April 2020

The Grand Tour was almost called Nigel on the basis that the show needed a name and Nigel is a name.

# FOREWORD
# by James May

To present a successful TV car show, you need three car bores. We pretend we're not, and that cars are an excuse for making an elaborate sit-com, but the truth is that we know a lot of banal facts about cars.

But not enough. Just as there are researchers and production staff behind the scenes of the show, there is also someone with the superpower equivalent of being boring about cars. That man is Richard Porter.

I could say that what Richard Porter doesn't know about cars isn't worth knowing, but that would be untrue. What Richard Porter *does* know about cars isn't worth knowing, as this book will demonstrate. He really can be quite dreary. At a party, he is not a man you find in the kitchen. You'll find him in the shed.

But we live in a modern world of inclusivity, where all triumphs and failures should be admitted and celebrated equally. This book should be seen as Richard Porter's confession; the unburdening of a soul tyrannised by facts about British saloon cars of the 1980s (for example). So read this book. You will be making a gesture of support.

But, Jesus, is it dull.

James May

# GENERAL

Volvo was the first car maker to fit six-figure odometers, as a symbol of its faith in the longevity of its cars.

*

Giorgetto Giugiaro was so angry with Alfa Romeo over changes it made to his design for the Alfetta GT and GTV (later to drop the Alfetta badge) that he took legal action to stop them using his name in relation to the car.

*

Only one Honda road car in history had a V8. It was the Honda Crossroad, which was a re-badged Land Rover Discovery mk1 sold exclusively in Japan.

*

The 2.5-litre flat four in the Lancia Gamma suffered from many problems including a lengthy timing belt supported by fragile belt tensioner bearings, a badly sited thermostat that would lead to overheating followed by head gasket failure and, most famously, a power steering pump bolted to one of the cylinder heads and driven by that bank's cambelt which meant that if you started the engine on a cold morning with the wheel not straight or steered too vigorously the pump was over-stressed by cold hydraulic fluid causing the cambelt on one half of the engine to jump while the belt on the other side carried on as normal and the resulting imbalance caused pistons to hit valves with catastrophic results. Little wonder one Italian publication described this engine as having "gross errors in design and construction".

*

When GM owned SAAB they also had a relationship with FIAT. As a result of this, and a desire to use Swedish brains in Trollhättan as an engineering consultancy, the four-wheel-drive system on the Fiat Panda 4x4 was engineered by SAAB.

For sensible economic reasons, the tuned-up HSV versions of Holden's 2006 VE Commodore had to be made on the same production line as regular Commodores but their fat tyres were too wide to fit down the guides on the assembly track and their front valances were too deep to make it off the ramp at the end. The solution was to build them with basic, unpainted Commodore bumpers and skinny, taxi-spec steel wheels then ship each car to a dedicated HSV facility where these low-spec items could be replaced with the correct trimmings.

*

In 1981 SEAT and FIAT signed an agreement to dissolve a working relationship that had been in place since SEAT was founded in 1950. Part of the agreement stipulated that SEAT could keep basing cars on existing FIAT models but there had to be greater differentiation in the designs. When SEAT announced the Strada-based Ronda in 1982, FIAT claimed it wasn't different enough and filed a lawsuit against its old partner in a Parisian court. In order to support its claim that it had made sufficient changes, the Spanish company presented to the court a black Ronda on which it had sprayed every SEAT-specific part bright yellow, including the entire interior. The court found in their favour.

*

The second-generation Renault Laguna was available with an optional built-in booster seat for children that flipped out from one side of the backseat base. The UK importer belatedly realised this was installed behind the driver's seat in right-hand-drive cars, potentially forcing parents to extract little kids into traffic on the offside of the car and hastily issued a recall for all Lagunas with this feature so they could have a new back seat fitted with the booster on the nearside. Fortunately for Renault this didn't cost a lot because the option wasn't well-known and very few people had ordered it.

*

The new Land Rover Defender has a very short rear overhang which is good for off-road performance but leaves no room to undersling the spare tyre which instead lives on the rear door, just as it did on the original. Unfortunately, the depth of the tyre means both rear lights aren't visible from a rear three-quarter angle, as required by legislation. That's why the Defender has a small pair of additional lights outboard on each side.

*

When Ian Callum was made Director of Design at Jaguar in 1999 he kept his previous job as Aston Martin design boss and set up a makeshift studio for Astons next to the Jag facility. As a result, two of the best looking cars in the world, the Aston DB9 and V8 Vantage, were designed in little more than a walled-off corner of a storage shed.

*

In the early 2000s Buick decided to buck its image as GM's maker of conservative cars for old people by introducing a radical interior concept in which all dials were replaced with a head-up display and all buttons and switches replaced with voice control, even the indicators, leaving the dashboard totally bare. The system, developed with Visteon, was called Quiet Servant. When Bob Lutz re-joined GM as vice president of product development in 2001 he was allowed to drive a prototype on public roads in Michigan. The Quiet Servant project was cancelled the following day.

The location for VW's huge Ehra-Lessien test track, opened in 1968, was chosen because at the time it was only six miles from the border with East Germany and therefore within a no-fly zone that would prevent people in small planes trying to spy on secret prototypes.

*

During Bravo/Brava development in the early nineties, Fiat boss Paulo Cantarella was keen to address the company's reputation for flimsiness and took a leading member of the quality control team to one side for a pep talk. "If this car squeaks and rattles," he said. "I'm going to physically harm you".

*

In the mid-nineties Jaguar engineers created a 'proof of concept' for a compact saloon by getting a BMW 3-series and fitting it with their own V8 and the suspension from an XJ40 to give a sense of what a smaller Jaguar should feel like. Unfortunately, Ford bosses were not convinced and imposed the Mondeo platform as the basis for what became the X-type.

*

In the eighties Rolls-Royce came up with a new, four cam, 5-litre V8 to replace the old pushrod 6.75-litre. For testing, they installed a prototype in a Chevrolet Caprice on the basis that it was big enough to take a large V8 and unfamiliar enough in the UK that most people wouldn't clock that the engine wasn't right if the bonnet had to be lifted in a public place. When the engine project got cancelled the Caprice mule was sold off. It's rumoured that this car still exists, hidden in a shed somewhere in the north of England.

The engine in the Nissan GT-R is canted slightly forward so that when it tips back under hard acceleration, it forms a perfect straight line with the shaft taking drive to the transaxle thereby minimising friction at the time when this would be most beneficial.

*

To coincide with the French release of the 1981 Bond film For Your Eyes Only in which Roger Moore outran some Peugeot 504 driving baddies in a 2CV (actually several stunt cars fitted with four-cylinder GS engines), Citroën announced a 500-off limited edition for its home market, featuring the same yellow paint as the movie cars, plus 007 graphics and bullet hole stickers across the panels. Citroën UK was interested in getting in on the Bond special edition action and asked a young, French-speaking marketing person to send a memo to head office in Paris. The message they wrote literally translated 'bullet holes' as 'trous de balle' which, unfortunately, is also French slang for something else. Hence Citroën head office received a message from their UK importer enthusing about the 007 limited edition covered in 'stickers of arseholes'.

*

Jaguar Land Rover's rotary gear selector that rises from the centre dash was introduced on the 2007 Jag XF only after engineers had ensured it could stand the most extreme mistreatment they could imagine which involved popping down to the local shop to buy a two litre bottle of Coke and pouring its entire contents into the mechanism.

The electric windows on modern Lexuses slow down as they near the top of their travel so that they slide smoothly and quietly into their seals, inspired by the Japanese etiquette for closing the sliding door on a room as unobtrusively as possible during a tea ceremony.

Geely, owner of Volvo and Lotus, wasn't always the Chinese car-making megacorp of today. In the nineties it was a refrigerator maker turned motorbike builder that decided to go into car manufacturing without the required permission from the Chinese government. Doing this required great stealth and ingenuity, which led company founder Li Shufu and a small gang of staff seconded from his motorbike factory to create the first panels by bashing metal over 'moulds' made from concrete because they couldn't afford proper panel presses. Once the bodyshells were hammered into shape they didn't have the durability test rigs of established car makers leaving one of the development team to open and close the prototype doors thousands of times by hand. Unfortunately, they forgot to do any testing in the rain and early examples leaked like rusty buckets, something that was only discovered after they had built the first 100 cars. Li decided to address this unfortunate mistake by hiring a road roller and personally crushing every single one of them.

The 1996 Mazda 121 was little more than a mk4 Ford Fiesta with some new badges and trimmings. This made it the only Mazda in history to be built in the UK. At the time Mazda offered a stronger warranty than Ford and it was therefore in its interests to make sure the cars weren't going to cost it, hence six Mazda staff were posted to the factory in Dagenham in order to keep an eye on things.

*

Peugeot reckoned the 1007, with its zany electric sliding doors, was such a cracking idea it would be able to sell 200,000 cars a year. In the end fewer than 125,000 were shifted in the entire five years the 1007 was on sale and the company lost an estimated €15,000 per car.

*

Chinese car buyers don't like the new car smell that is prized in the west. As a result, Chinese car companies work hard to eliminate it which has led Geely to launch a new car, the Icon, in which no glue is used in the construction of the interior.

*

The 2017 refresh of the Range Rover Sport introduced a more prominent rear spoiler which was tested to ensure it stayed in place at 80mph in reverse. The car itself can't do this, but many new Land Rovers are shipped on open train transporters and sometimes the cars are loaded on arse first. Land Rover realised the spoiler had to be strong enough to take the pressure of travelling backwards at high speed or it would be faced with trainloads of damaged cars.

*

When Ford engineers told Cosworth they wanted 200 horsepower from a Pinto-based 2-litre engine for what became the Sierra Cosworth, the engine maker replied that they might struggle… to keep the power *down* to that level.

*

In 2019 the Peugeot 405 entered production in Azerbaijan thanks to a new deal with local car maker, Khazar. Confusingly, this light update of a car first launched in 1987 is now called the Peugeot Khazar 406.

*

After the reveal of the mk4 Golf, Bob Lutz asked VW overlord Ferdinand Piëch how he had achieved the car's impressively tight shutlines and panel fits. Piëch replied that he had simply called the people responsible into his office and told them they had six weeks to make it happen or they would be fired.

*

Rover never managed to make gas turbine engines work in cars, but one of their gas turbine designs did sterling service in the B2 variant of the Avro Vulcan where it provided auxiliary electrical power.

*

In 2001 the Queen took delivery of a brand-new Land Rover Defender 110, specially built for her with a V8 engine and automatic gearbox. Shortly afterwards the car was returned to the factory with a personal request from the then 75-year-old sovereign; would they mind awfully changing the gearbox to a manual?

*

When Proton released its first car in 1985, the media in Malaysia was forbidden by government decree from saying anything critical about it.

# TEN CARS WITH UNUSUALLY SHORT LIVES

Buick Reatta
On sale 1988, production ended 1991

Chrysler TC by Maserati
On sale 1989, production ended 1990

Fiat 124 Spider
On sale 2016, production ended 2019

Leyland P76
On sale 1973, production ended 1974

Lotus Elan
On sale 1990, production ended (for the first time) 1992

Mercedes-Benz Vaneo
On sale 2002, production ended 2005

Mercedes-Benz X-class
On sale 2018, production ended 2020

Smart ForFour mk1
On sale 2004, production ended 2006

Suzuki X-90
On sale 1995, production ended 1997

Talbot Tagora
On sale 1981, production ended 1983

After the Second World War a commission of British industrialists led by car-making magnate Sir William Rootes was invited to inspect the ravaged Volkswagen factory in Wolfsburg and the car design it was built to manufacture. Upon returning to the UK Rootes filed a report in which he wrote, "The vehicle does not meet the technical requirements of a motor car. As regards performance and design it is quite unattractive to the average motor car buyer. It is too ugly and noisy - a car like this will remain popular for two or three years, if that. To build the car commercially would be a completely uneconomic enterprise." The Volkswagen Beetle went on to sell 21.5m cars over a life of 57 years. The Rootes Group no longer exists.

The Japanese market version of the Honda Concerto had a different front suspension (and, as a result, a different floorpan) to models sold in Europe. This came about because the car was a joint project with Rover whose engineers insisted that the car should have MacPherson struts at the front for cost and packaging reasons. Honda accepted that Rover knew more about Euro suspension tuning than it did, but wanted to maintain its devotion to engineering purity in the home market by giving Japanese cars double wishbones at the front instead.

*

The Australian Design Rules are stringent, Aussie-specific regulations all cars must meet to be sold down under and include, among other things, uncommonly tough stipulations about where the speedometer can be relative to a driver's line of sight. As a result of this, first- and second-generation BMW Minis sold in Australia had a speedometer mounted behind the steering wheel and the massive central speedo used in the rest of the world became a weirdly enormous rev counter.

*

During development of the V8-engined, rear-drive MG ZT 260, engineers noticed an undesirable amount of axle tramp from the back under hard acceleration. Rather than crunching numbers in a super computer to find the root of the problem, they lashed a prototype to the walls of the R&D workshop, got someone to light up the tyres in an extended burnout and made some poor sod slide under the back of the car to have a look at what was going on. The problem was solved by the unusual addition of a third damper in the middle of the axle.

Soon after Triumph Stag production ended in 1977 it became clear that the TR7 was tanking and the yet-to-be-launched four-seat Lynx coupé was going to be aborted. To salvage their sports car reputation BL hatched a plan to put the Stag back into production, this time using the Rover V8 engine. The idea was abandoned when it was found that some of the body tooling had already been scrapped.

*

Purists were aghast when Lotus fitted electric windows to the Elise, but the motorised system was actually lighter than the hand cranked set-up.

*

Gordon Murray had such confidence in the strength of the McLaren F1 that he asked to sit in the car during its mandatory 30mph crash test only to be thwarted when the authorities said no. The car performed so well in the test that, had the front lights not smashed, it would have been in a fit state to be driven home.

*

In the mid-seventies Sweden sold 1000 Volvos to North Korea. The Pyongyang government took the cars, and a load of Scandinavian industrial equipment, but never paid for them. As a result, Sweden still sends North Korea a twice-yearly bill for over $300 million.

*

Many of the body tools for the DeLorean DMC-12 ended up at the bottom of the Irish Sea after the receivers sold them for scrap and they were bought by a company that used them as weights for commercial fishing nets.

Chevrolet never sold a 1983 Corvette. The brand new C4 'Vette was supposed to be introduced in 1982 as an '83 model year car but the project ran so late Chevy skipped a year and finally launched it later in 1983 for the '84 model year. One of 43 pilot-build '83 models survived and is now in the National Corvette Museum in Bowling Green, Kentucky.

*

The E39 BMW M5 was the first M5 to be made on the regular 5 Series production line rather than hand built by the M division.

*

Nissan wanted every GT-R to look good for years to come so it created a 'cushion coat' layer over the paint that was designed to absorb the impact of flying stones, lessening the chances of the paintwork getting chipped. The effectiveness of this technology was developed using a prototype bonnet, an air rifle and a very large bag of peanuts.

*

During the energy crisis of the mid-seventies General Motors tried to buy back the tooling for the all-aluminium Buick V8 it had sold to Rover. The Americans wanted a smaller and more efficient engine as gasoline got more expensive but the British weren't for selling. They did offer to flog GM complete engines but the numbers didn't stack up.

*

The aluminium monocoques of modern Jaguars, starting with the X350 XJ of 2003, are descendants of experimental projects conducted in the early eighties by Alcan and BL's advanced research unit under original Range Rover designer Spen King. These projects included the BL ECV3 experimental car and a one-off aluminium-bodied MG Metro. King's far-sighted department, based at BL's Warwickshire proving ground, was called Gaydon Technology and known colloquially within the company as 'GayTech'.

*

When Aston did a deal to use Mercedes electronics it didn't like the harshness of the standard Benz warning tones and commissioned a company to come up with new, more British noises. The seat belt warning was given particular attention so that, according to Aston, it sounded "suggestive rather than demanding".

*

Until the end of its life in 1990 every new Citroën 2CV bodyshell still carried the tabs for the canvas bootlid that had ceased to be an option in the 1950s.

*

The Peugeot 1007 featured an interlock so that when the fuel filler flap was popped you couldn't open the sliding door on that side of the car to prevent it smashing into the pump handle. Fine on Euro models because the filler was on the driver's side. Annoying for UK cars where it meant a passenger couldn't escape from the car while it was being filled, even if they really wanted a wee or a bag of Revels.

*

In February 1980 BL boss Michael Edwardes was due to give a speech to the Birmingham Chamber of Commerce and Industry. Days earlier the company had dismissed infamous union convenor Derek "Red Robbo" Robinson and the BL workforce was about to vote on whether to accept this or to put management in an untenable situation by demanding his reinstatement via a strike that would bring the company to its knees. Edwardes wrote two speeches, one cheerily predicting a brighter future for BL, the other bluntly stating that all was lost and announcing that the company would be closed down. Just 15 minutes before Edwardes set off for the Chamber of Commerce news came through that the workers had voted overwhelmingly against strike action over Robinson's dismissal and the speech announcing BL's demise was torn up.

*

In the mid-sixties Ford spent ten times as much re-engineering an existing gearbox to add synchromesh to first gear ahead of using it in the Cortina as they did commissioning Cosworth to create a V8 engine for racing. The engine became the DFV which powered nine world titles and dominated F1 for 15 years.

*

When Austin Rover stopped making the Morris Ital in 1984 they put the tooling into storage. In 1994, they managed to sell it to Chengdu Auto Works of China.

*

During development of the first Cortina, Ford hired a former aircraft stress engineer to apply his knowledge to the bodyshell design. He was able to remove 150lb of steel from the shell compared to an equivalent body made with previous engineering techniques which meant that, at average Cortina production rates, Ford saved 75 tonnes of steel every day.

*

During the Italian Grand Prix it's often possible to see an old Ferrari 348 lurking at one of the marshalling posts. The car was a gift from Gerhard Berger to CEA Squadra Corse, the organisation that marshalls Italian races, as a thank you for saving his life after a massive accident during the 1989 San Marino Grand Prix.

*

In the world of Chevy V8s, the biggest small-block is bigger than the smallest big-block (400cu in/6.6 litres v 348cu in/5.7 litres).

*

During development of the GT-R a Nissan director raised questions about the car's run-flat tyres. Project boss Kazutoshi Mizuno put him in the passenger seat of a prototype, asked a development driver to take him on a hot lap and then before they set off let all the air out of one of the tyres. When the man came back in one piece he agreed that run-flat tyres were a good idea.

*

For 26 years lower-powered Minis came with drum brakes all round. This was fine as long as you remembered that drums don't work as well in reverse as they do going forwards. One person who forgot this was the wife of Austin Rover's boss man, causing her to smash backwards into a wall. Shortly after this incident all Minis got front disc brakes as standard.

*

The all-new Jaguar XJ6 of 1986 had a single windscreen wiper because chief engineer Jim Randle was a Citroën fan and wanted a futuristic CX vibe for his new car.

*

In the early stages of developing the SD1, Rover engineering boss Spen King had concerns that a live rear axle wouldn't be adequate for a new luxury car. Engineers convinced him otherwise by getting a P6 3500, fitting it with the live back axle from a Vauxhall Ventora, and taking him for a drive.

In 1966 Volkswagen commissioned Porsche to develop a new small car that it hoped would broaden its horizons beyond the ancient, if profitable, Beetle. The result was project EA266, a radical mid-engined three-door with its engine laid flat under the back seat. After five years work and £300 million spent, VW got as far as ordering the body tooling before realising it was a terrible idea. The handling was skittish, the interior was hot and noisy, the access to the engine was terrible, and every time it needed a service a mechanic would have to remove the back seat which, testing had proved, risked getting the cushion covered in oily fingerprints. EA266 was a disaster in waiting. In September 1971 VW got a new boss who was in the job a mere two weeks before he cancelled the entire project and told Porsche to destroy everything to do with it, including the 50 running prototypes. This was taken care of by running over them with a Leopard tank. One escaped and now lives in VW's museum.

Many years ago a homeless man wondered into the Bristol Cars showroom in Kensington and asked to be shown around one of the cars on display. The showroom staff humoured him, listing the car's specs and answering his questions until eventually he announced that he would like to order one, but only if they could make it the same colour as a small, blue saucepan which he produced from a carrier bag. Of course we can, sir, laughed the staff politely. "I'll leave that with you then," muttered the man, handing them the saucepan and walking off the premises. A few hours later a lady arrived asking if she could write the deposit cheque for the new car just ordered by her boss, the eccentric billionaire who liked to see how staff in ritzy places reacted if he came in dressed like a tramp. Bristol got his business for being the only place that gave him the time of day and he duly collected his new car, sprayed the same colour as an old saucepan. The company later took the car back into stock and advertised it for sale, listing the colour as Saucepan Blue.

Soon after BMW bought Rover Group in 1994, micro-moustached product development boss Wolfgang Reitzle arrived from Germany to make his initial examination of the forthcoming second-generation Range Rover. In front of nervous Rover management in the presentation room Reitzle climbed into the driver's seat of a pre-production car, put an airline sleep mask over his eyes, and spent five minutes silently feeling every single part of the interior within reach. He then got out of the car and wrote a 70-point list of all the areas he wanted to be improved.

*

The engine for the MG Metro Turbo was developed by Lotus.

*

Arjeplog, the epicentre of winter testing for many car makers, was first 'discovered' by two Opel engineers on an endurance test drive across Scandinavia. They reckoned the area's many frozen lakes would be perfect for building cold weather test tracks but to make sure this was safe they made a second visit with an example of their biggest, heaviest saloon which they pushed onto the ice with no one inside. When it didn't fall through the surface they knew they were onto something.

*

In the late eighties Mazda set up a separate Japan-only sub-brands called Autozam and Eunos, catering for customers with 'European' tastes who liked 'fun' cars. As well as selling the MX-5 and some of Mazda's wackier works like the AZ-1, MX-3, Cosmo and Xedos 6, stand-alone Autozam dealers sold Lancias and, from 1991 until 1996, the dedicated Eunos dealer network sold Citroëns.

In the mid-sixties the German press began taking pot-shots at Volkswagen for its over-reliance on the aging Beetle. Despite being hugely profitable at the time, VW was stung by this criticism and took the unusual step of inviting a pack of journalists into its R&D centre to show them 35 different prototypes of new cars it was working on. The move was self-defeating since all of these cars were rear-engined and air-cooled, just like the Beetle, and were also obsolete, painting a picture of a company that really was stuck in rut.

*

The clever and complicated Flex7 folding seat system in the first Vauxhall Zafira was engineered by Porsche.

*

The Jaguar C-X16 concept, first shown at the 2011 Frankfurt motor show as a preview of the F-type, was able to move under its own steam because underneath the slick and shiny exterior it was a sawn-up 57-plate Jag XK that had been hauled out of the R&D boneyard.

*

Volkswagen bought the Auto Union group purely for its new factory in Ingolstadt because they needed more room to make Beetles and expressly told the company not to waste its time developing any new models. Audi engineers ignored this and secretly created the first 100 saloon. They later won over management with the excellence of the prototype and the car was released in 1968 to such acclaim that, ironically, VW ended up making it in their Wolfsburg plant, as well as in Ingolstadt, to keep up with demand.

*

The aerodynamics of the Ford Sierra were refined in the Mercedes-Benz wind tunnel in Stuttgart.

When comical pay driver Taki Inoue left his native Japan for the first time and flew to England hoping to break into motorsport, the information desk at Heathrow misunderstood his request to find a good place for racing and put him on a coach to Newmarket race course. He later described inadvertently arriving at one of the UK's leading horse racing venues as "very disaster". Inoue subsequently became famous for getting run over by the marshalling car during the Hungarian Grand Prix and trying to blame his piss-poor driving on having toothache. However, his greatest humiliation was when one of his wealthy benefactors came to a grand prix and announced that he wanted Michael Schumacher's autograph. The only way for Inoue to get it was to go into the public area outside the paddock during a Schumacher meet 'n' greet and line up with all the punters until, upon reaching the front of the queue, he was able to ask for an autograph from a man he would be racing with the following day, albeit at completely opposite ends of the pack.

# TEN CARS THAT HAD CONVERTIBLE VERSIONS WHICH REACHED THE RUNNING PROTOTYPE STAGE BUT NEVER ENTERED PRODUCTION

Alfa Romeo GT
BMW 8 Series (E31)
BMW M5 (E34)
Dodge Challenger (2008)
Mercedes-Benz 190E
Porsche 901
Porsche 928
Vauxhall Chevette
Volkswagen Corrado
Volvo 480 ES

The Austin Ambassador was never made in left-hand-drive. At least one prototype was built, but production was right-hand-drive only. It's not completely clear why this was so, but there's a clue in the reaction of the man from Leyland Italia when he was shown the car for the first time. Please, he is said to have begged, do not send me this car.

*

In the early 2000s the team responsible for the Land Rover Defender was basically two bored blokes in an office in Solihull. With not much else to do, they came up with a cost-effective plan to address the car's famous lack of elbow room by splicing the shell down the middle and letting in some extra metal to the benefit of interior space. By deleting the wheel arch extensions, the overall width of the thing was no greater than the standard car and the tin bashers on the Defender line who gave it a trial run reckoned it would be easy to do in production. The cunning scheme was sunk because they couldn't get the funds for all the other parts – glass, grille, dash – that would also need to be made wider.

*

The second-generation BMW Mini has something in common with the Morris Ital. The body engineering for both cars was handled by Ital Design.

*

In 1979 SAAB and Lancia agreed to co-operate on a new large car project which would become, with the addition of Fiat and Alfa Romeo, the Type 4 platform. In those early days it didn't take long for the different corporate cultures to clash, such as when Lancia invited SAAB engineers to Italy to witness the first crash test of a prototype. After the car had hit the concrete block the

SAAB team solemnly declared that "there is much work to do". Which was strange, because the Lancia team proudly declared the results to be "perfect".

*

The fifth generation Chevrolet Camaro of 2010 might have seemed as American as an apple pie with a gun in it, but most of its design and engineering was completed by Holden in Australia and it was assembled in Canada.

*

The small and secretive team tasked with developing the second-generation Ford GT didn't want anyone to guess that they were working on a 650 horsepower mid-engined supercar so they gave the project the most unlikely-sounding codename possible; Petunia.

*

In 1957 Chevrolet introduced a new option called the Flame Out Ashtray. At the touch of a button the system used the vacuum effect from the engine to suck cigarette butts and ash from the ashtray into a glass bottle under the dashboard. It was so-named because the vacuum extinguished lit cigarettes, thereby eliminating the risk of an ashtray fire. As it turned out, most Chevrolet customers weren't too concerned about the risk of ashtray fire, uptake on the option was small and after four model years it was deleted.

*

The Sunbeam Tiger was a version of the Alpine with a meaty Ford V8 in place of the Alpine's four cylinder. In order to squeeze in the larger engine, a burly man on the production line would step into the engine bay and bash at the inner wings with a large hammer to get the required clearance before the engine was lowered into place. When Chrysler completed their purchase of

Rootes Group in 1967 the Ford V8 had to go and attempts to fit an equivalent Chrysler engine were thwarted because the burly man simply couldn't bash enough metal out of the way.

*

Late in the development of the Rover 75, overlords at BMW made British engineers re-design the roof panel at a cost of over £1 million because they had noticed what they considered to be an unacceptably visible seam within the sunroof aperture.

*

The four-wheel-drive version of the sportiest Peugeot 405, the Mi16x4, used Citroën hydropneumatic suspension, but only on the rear axle.

*

The Volvo 340 could have been a BMW or an Audi. Before Volvo bought into DAF, the Dutch company was developing the car alone as project P900, to be called DAF 77 in production, but needed a partner to see it through. Talks were held with VAG and BMW, both of whom would have adopted the design as their own, before Volvo bought a third of DAF in 1972, bagging the P900 as their entry-level car.

*

The Ferrari California was originally developed by Maserati. When it was belatedly realised that a bespoke all-aluminium shell and Ferrari-made V8 would be impossible to sell profitably at Maserati prices the car was adopted by Ferrari. FCA boss Sergio Marchionne gave the game away at the 2017 Geneva motor show when he admitted that the California "had the hardest time of seeing itself as a full-blown Ferrari".

The short-wheelbase Audi Sport Quattro used the more upright windscreen pillars from the Audi 80 saloon, rather than the coupé, to give more headroom for occupants in crash helmets.

\*

When Ford started on-road development of the Sierra by installing its chassis hardware under a fleet of Cortinas, they encountered an unexpected problem. From the back, the new car's semi-trailing arm rear end made it look like the Cortina's normal live axle had collapsed, causing development drivers to get stopped by concerned motorists and the police. Ford engineers solved the problem by ensuring every Sierra mule was followed closely by a chase car, or was towing a small trailer so the back axle couldn't be seen.

\*

The Dodge Viper's V10 was engineered by Lamborghini.

\*

The Peugeot 309 was styled in Coventry as a replacement for the Talbot Horizon, to be called the Arizona. The car was almost ready when, in 1985, PSA decided to kill off Talbot leading to a hasty re-badging.

\*

A car's fuel filler location is usually determined by its country of origin and the side of the road they drive on, as a hangover from when petrol was sold at the side of the road and it made sense to have the filler kerbside.

\*

Jaguar's AJ126 engine, the supercharged V6 used in Jags and Land Rovers since 2013, is the larger AJ133 V8 with two of the cylinders blanked off and shorter cylinder heads mounted on the same length block.

In 1987 CAR magazine ran a cover story about a top secret new Porsche, illustrated by some murky, super long lens pictures of a mysterious black car on test. But the car papped wasn't a forthcoming production car, it was actually the PEP (Porsche Experimental Prototype), an unusual test bed for chassis designs built around a central aluminium monocoque to which modular tubular-framed subframes could be bolted to test out different suspension designs. Track width could be changed and so could wheelbase, thanks to a telescopic propshaft within the four-wheel-drive system that took power from a 911's flat six mounted in the middle. The car could be run with four-wheel-drive, rear-wheel-drive or even just power to the front wheels and the weight distribution could be tweaked by adding ballast in strategic areas beneath the crude fibreglass skin. It seemed like a brilliant idea, but it didn't quite work out as well as its creators had hoped. Engineers admitted that it was too crude and rough to get a good feeling for which set-ups and configurations worked most effectively and soon after its starring appearance in CAR the PEP was abandoned.

*

During development of the 2007 DBS, Aston Martin engineers were struggling to find the right tyre for the car until they chanced upon a special not-for-sale Pirelli PZero confected exclusively for the DBS stunt cars used in the Bond film, *Casino Royale*. Pirelli agreed to put it into production and this tyre, coded AMS, ended up being used not only on the DBS but also on the Jaguar XKR-S and the rear wheels of some F-types.

*

When Porsche launched the facelifted 928 S4 for 1987

the larger rear spoiler was hinged to flip forward, making it easier to clean the back of the car. By 1988 they clearly decided this was an unnecessary luxury and the hinges were deleted.

*

According to research conducted by BMW in 2010, four out of five 1 Series owners thought their car was front-wheel-drive.

*

When the Peugeot 405 was launched in 1987, left-hand-drive models were built in France and right-hand-drive cars in the UK. But steering wheel position wasn't the only difference between 405s from the two factories because French-built cars had their radio aerial on the roof whereas British-made cars had an old-fashioned retractable aerial on the passenger-side rear wing (until the facelift of 1993 when British cars' aerials moved to the roof). The reason for this is lost in the mists of time, though it could have been because UK customers loved sunroofs where mainland Euro buyer were less keen and a wing-mounted aerial was easier to install on the production line, negating the need to fit the wiring around a sunroof aperture and mechanism.

*

The Porsche 959 has a six-speed gearbox but the lowest forward gear is labelled G (for Gelände, or 'terrain' in German, also what the G in Mercedes G-Class stands for) and is a super low gear for off-road use. In normal road driving you set off in the gear labelled 1, which is down and back like a dog leg 'box.

*

The Lancia Delta was sold in Sweden, Finland and Norway as the SAAB Lancia 600.

Lexus claimed the LFA needed a digital rev counter because its V10 gained and shed revs so quickly an analogue gauge couldn't keep up.

*

When the Ford Pinto developed a reputation for bursting into flames if rear-ended, radio ads for the car were edited to remove the unfortunate tagline, "Pinto leaves you with that warm feeling".

*

The 1999-2006 Kia Sedona people carrier was available with Rover's 2.5-litre KV6 engine.

*

The Renault Avantime's name was a contraction of the French for 'ahead of time', which was ironic since it went on sale over a year late because of problems engineering its enormous and complicated doors.

*

In 1977 General Motors launched a diesel engine option in an attempt to offer improved fuel economy. This 5.7-litre V8 made 125 horsepower until 1980 when the power output was downgraded to 105 horsepower.

*

At the start of the project that became the Maestro, BL engineers under Spen King decided the car would be best with a simple, VW-style torsion beam rear axle. To validate this belief they went to a Birmingham Volkswagen dealer and bought a Polo back axle which they installed on an Allegro. Satisfied that it worked, they then copied the design, beefed it up to take the weight of the larger Maestro, and signed it off for production.

*

Jaguar was so keen to keep the look of the XJ40 a secret before its launch in 1986 that for five years all prototype and pre-production cars wore a comprehensive fibreglass disguise kit which weighed 90 kilos and cost £1000 a set, equivalent to three grand today. The camouflage evolved as development went on, ending with a third generation camo kit that allowed the boot and bonnet to be opened without removing any of the false panels and maintained the same drag coefficient as the un-disguised car.

*

Between 1996 and 1999 GM built 2234 examples of its radical EV1 electric car before shutting down the production line. Since the EV1 was only available on a lease, all the cars belonged to GM and when the leases ended the cars were taken to GM's Arizona proving ground where they were crushed.

*

When the Mastercard Lola team made its debut at the 1997 Australian Grand Prix with a car that had spent precisely zero hours in the wind tunnel, their fastest qualifying effort was 11 seconds off the pace.

*

The 1975 Lancia Montecarlo became famous for locking its front wheels, thanks to rear-biased weight distribution and a servo that worked on the front brakes alone. The problem was so severe that in February 1978 Montecarlo production was paused and the car didn't return to sale until January 1980 when it was re-introduced with a revised braking system. The main 'revision' was the removal of the servo.

Until 1967 Sweden drove on the left-hand-side of the road. After years of planning, Sunday 3 September 1967 was designated Dagen H ("H day") when the country would switch to driving on the right. The H stood for Högertrafikomläggningen or 'the right hand traffic diversion'. At 1am roads were closed to all but essential traffic and at 4:50am anything still on the street was required to stop, carefully switch sides and then wait until the stroke of 5am and the climax of a countdown on the radio which then announced that Sweden now drove on the right. Other traffic was allowed back onto the roads in most places at 6am. Making the change involved re-drawing road markings, re-configuring junctions and changing road signs. It also involved a massive publicity campaign, including a promotional song called Keep To The Right, Svensson. In today's money, the whole project cost over £450m.

In the mid-eighties Lotus was commissioned by its General Motors overlords to develop its active suspension technology for the mid-engined, four-wheel-drive Corvette Indy concept car which GM wanted to turn from a static show car into a running tech showcase. To get everything working well, Lotus engineers needed another mid-engined, four-wheel-drive car in which they could install their active systems. That's why they bought one of 200 Peugeot 205 T16 homologation specials. In fact, they bought two. One was heavily modified to take the active suspension and a four-wheel-steering system. The other was kept standard to provide a benchmark for the improvements offered by the active car. Once the technology mule was working to Lotus's satisfaction both cars were shipped to GM in Michigan where they disappeared inside their engineering centre only to appear unexpectedly more than 30 years later when they crossed the block at a 2018 Barrett-Jackson auction in Scottsdale, Arizona.

## TEN CARS MADE NOT WHERE
## YOU MIGHT THINK

Audi e-tron – Brussels, Belgium
Ford Puma – Craiova, Romania
Honda NSX – Marysville, Ohio, USA
Jaguar I-Pace – Graz, Austria
Jeep Renegade – Melfi, Italy
Land Rover Defender – Nitra, Slovakia
Mini Countryman – Born, Netherlands
SEAT Ateca – Kvasiny, Czech Republic
Toyota Supra – Graz, Austria
Volvo S90 – Daqing, China

In 1994 BMW bought Rover Group for £800m. In 2000 they sold Land Rover to Ford for £1.85 billion and Rover to four Midlands businessmen for £10.

*

The Cadillac Allanté, launched in 1986, was built with the help of what GM called 'The Allanté Airbridge'. This was three specially adapted Boeing 747 freighters which shipped US-made floorpans, wiring looms, air-con systems and seats to Pininfarina in Italy where they were mated with bodyshells and interiors before the trimmed shells were flown back to the United States to receive their engines and suspensions making the 'production line' for this not-very-successful car insanely expensive and over 9000 miles long.

*

The first wind tunnel tests of the Vauxhall Calibra gave an unremarkable Cd figure of 0.33. The car's eventual, headline grabbing Cd of 0.26 was largely achieved not by tweaking the front of the car but by increasing the taper of the rear end (although only the base model had the 0.26 Cd, other models recorded a Cd of 0.29).

*

The Abarth 124 Spider was available with an optional matt black bonnet, but how this was added depended on where you lived. For American customers the bonnet was painted matt black once the cars arrived on US soil. In Europe the effect was achieved with a matt black wrap applied in Italy. And for customers in Australia and New Zealand there was no matt black bonnet option because the cars came straight from the Mazda factory in Japan where all 124s were made and Fiat didn't have the local facility to change the bonnet colour.

The estate version of the Citroën ID, introduced in 1958, had a split tailgate with a second rear number plate mounted horizontally on top of the lower section so that it became visible when the boot was open allowing the car to be driven legally with the lower tailgate down.

*

The 1986 Audi 80 was criticised for having a small boot. Audi bosses had signed off such a thing because they assumed there would be an estate version, only for this to be deleted from the original product plan (finally arriving with the major facelift in 1991). In an attempt to hide the problem, Audi dealers were given a set of fitted luggage to put in their showroom display models which was designed to make the boot look bigger.

*

What do the Alfa Romeo 145/146, the Citroën Visa and the original Fiat Panda have in common? All were offered simultaneously with lengthways AND crossways engines, in the same shell and driving the same wheels. In the Alfa's case, the longitudinal engine was the old boxer from the Alfasud and the transverse ones were the newer Twin Spark units. Base model Visas had a flat twin mounted longways, other models used in-line fours installed across the car. The Panda (and for that matter the Cinquecento) could be had at launch with an inline twin or a crossways straight four.

*

During the 2002 US Grand Prix, Pedro de la Rosa's disastrous Jaguar R3 lunched its gearbox and then caught fire for good measure. But the Spanish driver's bad luck didn't end there because, after dumping the car, he hopped the nearest barrier and fell into a small river.

When the Ford Model T was introduced in 1908 it was available in several colours. In 1914 the quest for greater mass production efficiency saw the colour palette reduced to just one which prompted Henry Ford to say, "Any customer can have a car painted any colour that he wants so long as it is black". In 1926 Ford started offering the Model T in other colours again.

*

BMW never planned to make an estate version of the E30 3-series until Max Reisböck, an engineer from their prototype workshop, bought a crashed 323i saloon and spent six months of his free time turning it into an estate in a friend's garage so he had a more practical car for his family. BMW bosses got wind of the project and liked it so much they adopted it for production using Reisböck's hand built one-off as the template.

*

During the programme to install Jaguar V8s in the third generation Range Rover in lieu of BMW engines, engineers tried fitting one car with Aston Martin's 5.9-litre V12. The engine went in, but there was no room to hook up the front driveshafts so this two-tonne, 450+ horsepower prototype was rear-wheel-drive only.

*

One of Ford's attempts to salvage disastrous Edsel sales was to buy 1000 ponies and send them out to showrooms in the hope it would make excitable kids drag their parents through the doors so a salesman could pounce. Each dealer ran a competition to give away their pony but most people didn't want or need a small horse in their house and took the offered alternative of $200 cash. As a result, most of the ponies ended up being shipped back to Ford head office in Detroit.

Land Rover hatched many schemes to make a new Defender but, until 2019, they always faltered because the sums didn't add up. One such plan, confected under Ford ownership, was to build a car based on the Ford Ranger chassis.

*

The Lincoln Town Car might seem quintessentially American but much of the second-generation model, launched in 1989, was engineered by IAD, an automotive consultancy based in Sussex. This made the Town Car the first US domestic market Ford to be engineered by an outside company.

*

Development of the four-wheel-drive version of the Lamborghini Diablo suffered a setback when, in 1992, the lorry carrying the only prototype on its way back from testing at Nardo was held up by thieves who made off with the truck and its contents. The lorry and the car were later recovered at the port in Brindisi.

*

Older Honda motors used to turn in the opposite direction to most other company's engines. Without looking at the cam cover logo you could tell whether a 1989-era Rover 200 had a Rover or a Honda engine by how it sat in the engine bay. Rover's K-series was mounted to the left with the gearbox on the right when viewed from the front. The Honda D-series was fitted over to the right with the gearbox on the left.

*

In 1983 Audi gave the ur-quattro a voice synthesizer system which used the smooth tones of Patrizia Lipp, the traffic and travel presenter on Radio Bayern.

Since the nineties cars with frameless door windows have automatically dropped the glass slightly when the door opens in order to clear the seals, but this feature was first seen on the Bristol 412 of 1975. Sadly for Bristol, they couldn't afford to patent the system.

*

The Citroën XM had a second rear screen inside the car so that people in the back seat didn't get a draught down their necks when the tailgate was opened.

*

During development of the new Mini, engineers at Rover were unhappy with the proposed electric power steering set-up and came up with an electro-hydraulic hybrid system that they believed would give more steering feel. To persuade management that this was a good idea, they cobbled together a demonstrator using an old Ford Mondeo.

*

The electric window switches in the Alfa 75 were mounted in the ceiling.

*

When BMW initiated a plan to install its V8 petrol engines in the P38a Range Rover, it also investigated the creation of a top-of-the-range model using the V12 from the 750i. At least two V12 prototypes were built, one of which became the personal runaround of precisely moustachioed engineering boss Wolfgang Reitzle, before the entire engine plan was abandoned and attention turned instead to the third-gen Range Rover project.

*

The Mercedes B-class Electric Drive used Tesla technology. Between 2009 and 2014 Daimler owned just under 10 percent of Tesla.

During development of the XJ40, Jaguar engineers responsible for one heavily camouflaged prototype got some chrome beading from an old Mini, bent it into the facsimile of the BMW 'kidney' grille and stuck it on the front before taking it to a well-known car testing environment. Word soon came through from Munich asking them to knock it off with their nonsense. Land Rover engineers pulled a similar stunt while winter testing the second-generation Range Rover, after learning that their company had just been bought by BMW. Sometime later, as if returning these favours, German engineers were papped in prototype E46 3 Series' with Rover grilles stuck to their noses.

*

The Smart Roadster had the same wheelbase as the 997-shape Porsche 911.

*

In 2001 MG Rover almost completed a deal with Matra to develop a re-skinned, Roverised version of the mk3 Renault Espace.

*

In the nineties kit car maker Banham bought the original moulds for the fibreglass shell of the Ford RS200 and adapted the bodywork to create a build-at-home version. To make this project feasible they needed to identify an affordable donor car of similar dimensions to an RS200 That's why Banham RS200s were front-engined, front-wheel-drive and based on the Austin Maestro.

*

The 2018 Porsche 935 'Moby Dick' homage exists because of Magnum ice creams. Porsche's motorsport people were talking to a business consultant about future strategy when discussion turned to Magnums as the first ice creams to be marketed to adults rather than children. From this the Porsche people were inspired to create a 'grown up' track day car, the circuit-only GT2 RS Clubsport, and wanted to offer it with a flatnose option only for the designer tasked with drawing some new wings to get carried away and re-do the entire car as a modern day Moby Dick. Since it was coming up to Porsche's 70th, they decided to build it as a birthday present to themselves.

*

The 2005 Aston Martin V8 Vantage was intended to be mid-engined and had reached the full-size styling model stage in this layout before Aston boss Ulrich Bez decided it was more appropriate for Astons to be front-engined. Another full-size clay model was made using the same design themes adapted for the change in engine location but giving away its past with vestigial intakes at the rear that were eventually removed for production.

*

The 1996 Volkswagen Polo Harlequin with its bizarre mis-matched panels was made by taking four completed cars (one red, one blue, one yellow and one green) into a workshop at the end of the production line where the panels could be swapped to a pre-set formula. The colour of the sills, rear three-quarter panel and roof gave away the colour of the 'base' car.

*

In the mid-seventies a British firm decided to import AMC Pacers from the US to the UK and convert them to right-hand-drive. This low-budget conversion was achieved by cutting the steering column, switching the wheel end to the other side of the car and then connecting the two parts with a chain running behind the bulkhead in the engine bay, while the brake pedal was linked to the servo via a long connecting rod. Another thing that made the three-door Pacer less-than-ideal for British motorists was the innovative asymmetric body design which, for Americans, meant a longer passenger door to aid access to the back seat but for the British meant a pointlessly massive driver's door. This was rendered even more inconvenient by the sheer size of the Pacer which had been designed to give Americans the handy length of a compact car with the prestigious width of something larger. For Britons that meant a car as long as a Hillman Hunter yet, at 6' 5" across, wider than any car made in Europe at the time.

*

The Subaru BRAT was never officially sold in Japan.

# NAMES

The sportiest version of the 1995 Rover 200 was going to be called the VVC in honour of the Variable Valve Control on its engine (known internally as 'Very Very Complicated'). The model name was changed to Vi late in the day after someone realised that VVC written in Rover's badge typeface looked like 'WC'.

*

In the mid-nineties Volvo decided to revamp the way it named its cars so that each saloon model name would start with an S and each estate with an F (for 'flexibility') followed by a single digit to indicate relative size. This system would be launched on the new Dutch-made medium sized cars, the S4 and F4. Badges were made, marketing materials had been printed and the names had been announced before Audi, which already made an S4, politely cleared its throat and told Volvo to think again. The solution was to add a zero to each model name making the saloon the S40 and the estate the… oh bugger. To dodge an angry call from Ferrari, Volvo estates adopted a V for versatility.

*

The original Fiat Panda wasn't named after an ursine shag-o-phobe but in honour of Empanda, the Roman goddess of asylum, charity and hospitality. It was originally going to be called the Rustica until this name met with a tepid reaction in market research. At the 2003 Geneva Show Fiat showed off a new small car which they called the Gingo until Renault strongly objected on the grounds that it sounded too much like Twingo. This car became the second-generation Panda.

*

The EV1 was the first car in General Motors' history to be badged as a GM.

In the late sixties Fiat introduced an internal system for identifying projects in which all engine codenames started X0 and all complete cars X1. The Fiat 128 kicked things off, being codenamed X1/1. These codes were generally for internal use only, with exception of a small mid-engined sports car that was to be called 128 Spider until late in the day when that name was dropped and the car was shoved into production wearing its internal codename, X1/9.

*

During development, the team responsible for the 2009 Jaguar XFR informally codenamed it 'Weapon Of Choice'.

*

When the Ferrari 365 GT/4 BB was released at the 1971 Paris Motor Show, the Italian company tried to suggest that the BB part of the name stood for 'Berlinetta Boxer'. This was a bit odd since Berlinetta, or 'little saloon', was usually used only on their front engine cars and the car's engine was a 180 degree V12, not a Boxer. Many years later designer Leonardo Fioravanti admitted to The Road Rat that the Berlinetta Boxer thing was another B-word; bollocks. The BB in the name was actually there because everyone on the design team had the hots for Brigitte Bardot.

*

The Vauxhall VX220 was codenamed 'Skipton' in the hope that anyone seeing or hearing the name of a gentle North Yorkshire market town wouldn't guess that Vauxhall was planning a mid-engined sports car. When they came to develop the turbocharged version they got a bit more dynamic and codenamed it 'Tornado'.

In 2001 Snoop Dogg pitched Cadillac to design a limited-edition car for them which he wanted to call the Snoop de Ville.

*

The original, informal codename for the 2007 Nissan GT-R was 'The Traction Master'.

*

The Citroën Saxo was sold in Japan as the Citroën Chanson because Honda owned the Saxo name. Chanson is French for 'song'.

*

Two British cars have been codenamed XX. The first was the saloon that became the Rover 800. The second was a TWR project to re-clothe the Jaguar XJ-S using design cues from the aborted XJ41 'F-type' project. When Jag passed on TWR's plan, the XX project evolved into the Aston Martin DB7.

*

In 1987 Austin Rover released a Metro special edition called, rather strangely, the Studio 2. It got its name because it was confected by the colour & trim department who were based in Studio 2 of the company's Canley design centre.

*

The Ford Capri was to be called the Colt until it was discovered that Mitsubishi had trademarked this name.

*

The Morris Marina was sold in the US, Canada and South Africa as the Austin Marina because Austin enjoyed better brand recognition in those countries.

*

The Audi 80 and 100 got their names because they had 80 and 100 horsepower respectively.

In the 1990s Rover Group started giving new car projects code names rather than numbers. Here are some of them.

- Adder - MG RV8
- Jewel – Rover 25
- Oyster – Rover 45
- Remus - Range Rover 'soft dash' facelift
- Romulus - Land Rover Discovery mk1 facelift
- Synchro - Rover 600
- Tex - Rover 400 Tourer
- Tomcat - Rover 200 Coupé
- Topaz – Rover 100 Cabriolet
- Tracer - Rover 200 Cabriolet
- Troy – Rover Mini Cabriolet

Mercedes-Benz's tradition of starting development codenames with a W (W124, W201, et al) dates back to 1922 and a system introduced by founding company, Daimler. The W stands for 'wagen', or 'car' in German. However, other codes are also used. Here's a list.

A = cabriolet with fabric roof
C = coupé
R = roadster
S = estate
V = saloon, long wheelbase
W = most standard models
X = SUV variant of another model
Z = extra long wheelbase, including rolling chassis' used to make hearses and six door saloons for funeral directors.

The second-generation Range Rover was initially developed under the codename 'Project Discovery'. When it was decided to give that name to the production version of the new mid-level Land Rover, launched in 1989, the Range Rover programme was changed to 'Project Pegasus' and later '38A' after the building in which the development team was based (sometimes merged together as P38A with P for Pegasus).

*

The Volkswagen Corrado was going to be called the Taifun, German for typhoon. The VR6 engine, installed in early Corrado prototypes (though it didn't make production in the car until later in its life) was labelled RV6 on the cam covers.

*

Humvee comes from HMMWV or High Mobility Multipurpose Wheeled Vehicle, the original US military title used on the tender documents for an all-in-one replacement for various light tactical vehicles.

*

The Vauxhall/Opel Cascada was named after the Spanish word for waterfall, yet in Spain the car was called the Opel Cabrio because 'cascada' was too close to 'cascado', which means tinny, worn-out and crap.

*

When the Citroën C15 was launched in the UK it was available only in red or white, labelled in the brochure as 'Van Rouge' or 'Van Blanc'.

*

The Suzuki Splash was sold as the Suzuki Ritz in India and Nepal because Ford owned the rights to the name Splash in those places.

Names considered for the original Ford Fiesta included Bobcat (its development codename), Bravo, Amigo and Model B. When Fiesta became the preferred choice Henry Ford had to ring GM's chairman to get permission because the name had previously been used on an Oldsmobile.

*

Aston Martin wanted to name a track-biased version of the V12 Vantage the GT3. Porsche got sniffy about this so at the last minute Aston upped the ante by calling it GT12 instead.

*

The RA badge given to hardcore, lightweight Subarus stands for 'Record Attempt' and was first used on a tricked-up Legacy RS Type, the first car to come out of the STI division, which was built for a 100,000 kilometre endurance trial in 1989.

*

BMW refers to the mid-life facelift of its models as an 'LCI' or 'Life Cycle Impulse'.

*

VW launched the up! with two special editions, the up! White and the up! Black. In other countries the two words in the name were the other way around but the UK importer had to firmly insist that it would struggle to sell a car called the 'Black up!'

*

Jaguar's XJ model designation is an abbreviation of eXperimental Jaguar.

*

The Ford Mondeo was almost called the Ford Lyrus.

The McLaren MP4-12C's name comes from the following things;

- MP4 - McLaren's prefix for all racing cars made after 1981, taken from Ron Dennis's old team, Project Four, and their sponsor, Marlboro, though changed to mean McLaren Project 4 when the two firms merged.
- 12 – Taken from McLaren's 'internal index of vehicle performance', an equation that uses factors including power, performance, weight and aerodynamics to return a number, in this case 12.
- C – Carbon fibre

When Mitsubishi UK badged versions of the Lancer Evolution VIII as 'FQ' to distinguish them from grey imports, head office in Japan asked what these letters stood for and were told it was 'Fine Quality'. This pleased them, and they never guessed that the British end actually meant FQ to stand for 'Fucking Quick'.

The Austin Metro got its name after a poll among BL staff which invited them to choose between Metro, Maestro and Match. Metro beat Maestro by 8599 votes to 8332. Before signing off on Metro, management had to get permission from train maker Metro-Cammell. Early cars were badged the miniMETRO, though not before prototype badges had been made up that reversed the capitalisation as 'MINImetro'.

*

When, in the mid-seventies, Ford wanted to splash the letters MPG across US adverts to emphasise the economy of its smaller models, Henry Ford had to personally get permission from agricultural co-operative, Maine Potato Growers.

*

The new Mini was originally codenamed R59 by Rover as a nod to the original which came out in 1959. BMW changed the code to R50 and R59 later became the internal designation of the Mini Roadster.

*

The first Mercedes M-Class was codenamed W163, the second W164, the third W166 and the fourth W167. W165 was skipped because it had already been used as the name for a V8-powered racing car design of 1939 which raced only once, in the Tripoli Grand Prix, where it came first and second.

*

Volkswagen didn't refer to its most famous product as the Beetle for the first 30 years of its life. The Beetle nickname (Käfer in German) was used in official literature for the first time in 1968.

# JAPANESE ACRONYMS
# AND ABBREVIATIONS

ATTESA
Advanced Total Traction Engineering System for All-
terrain

BRAT
Bi-drive Recreational All-terrain Transporter

i-MiEV
innovative – Mitsubishi innovative Electric Vehicle

Liana
Life In A New Age

MIVEC
Mitsubishi Innovative Valve timing Electronic Control

NSX
New Sportscar Unknown World (where X = unknown)

RAV4
Recreational Activity Vehicle 4-wheel-drive

STI
Subaru Tecnica International

VTEC
Variable Valve Timing & Lift Electronic Control

# DESIGN

Ford wanted the interior of the first Focus to be an interesting and tactile place. That's why the heater control knobs were made of an unusual rubbery material which came about after a keen windsurfer on the design team brought in his neoprene wetsuit and suggested controls could be made of the same material. This turned out to be impractical, so a rubber coating was developed to replicate the texture.

*

The 2007 facelift of the first aluminium bodied Jaguar XJ was surprisingly sporty, what with its mesh grilles, deep bumpers, side vents and boot spoiler. Designers meant for this to be the R version alone, with a more sedate style for other models, but management liked the look so much they insisted every model in the range had the sporty trimmings.

*

The infamous rear wing on the Sierra Cosworth went through 92 iterations to get right, aerodynamically speaking. It could have been more effective if it had extended six inches further back, but that would have been illegal on a road car unless the back bumper was extended to match and Ford couldn't justify spending the money on a new bumper as well.

*

At Jaguar's new design facility in Gaydon, opened in 2019, the main studios are numbered 3 and 4. There are no studios 1 or 2 in the building. They were the studios at the old Jag design centre in Whitley.

*

For many years Rover's colour & trim boss was a man called Martin Peach.

The fake leather grain embossed into plastic car interior parts is taken from a real piece of hide. For the second-generation Range Rover, the designers searched long and hard for the right faux texture and finally found it on the underbelly of an antelope.

*

In the eighties many car companies relied on a firm in Cambridgeshire to turn their finished clay styling bucks into highly realistic full-scale fibreglass models which could be used for management presentations and customer clinics before a new design was committed to production. Naturally, this company took great steps to make sure their windowless facility was extremely secure but they forgot to consider the possibility of a cheeky spy climbing onto the roof and taking photos through the skylights of all the top secret future cars being rendered in fibreglass below. The photos themselves were legally dubious to publish, but they could be used to create uncannily accurate drawings of forthcoming models which is why, for example, some of the renderings in the CAR magazine Scoop '85! supplement of late 1984 were uncommonly accurate.

*

The radically cab-forward 300M of 1999 was a hit for Chrysler, leading GM management to ask its designers why they couldn't style something as attention grabbing. The designers' response was to park a 300M in the massive GM design centre viewing room covered in over 90 Post-it notes highlighting every single area in which the car didn't meet GM's restrictive internal design rules.

Since 2006 Vauxhalls (and Opel equivalents) have had a cartoon shark moulded into the plastic somewhere in the interior. The practise was started by designer Dietmar Finger who was given responsibility to design some plastic ribs for the side of the glovebox moulding in the forthcoming Corsa D and was encouraged by his young son to "just draw a shark". The shark made it into production and started a game amongst other interior designers to hide a shark somewhere within each new model they designed. In the Adam there were sharks inside the door bins. The Crossland X has one on the side of the flip out cubby by the driver's knee. In the Astra the shark is moulded into the underside of the cupholder insert.

*

In 1983 Citroën held a design shootout for what would become the XM. Management chose a proposal from Bertone which everyone agreed looked way better than offerings from Marcello Gandini and PSA's in-house studios. It's only when Citroën's designers and engineers went off to make the design suitable for production that they discovered why the Bertone car seemed so much more attractive; the Italians had ignored the engineering package they'd been sent and tweaked the proportions to make the car look better, even though it could never be built like that because the mechanical parts and important things like the heater simply wouldn't fit. Dragging everything back to the right hard points while preserving the look that management liked so much was such a headache that they had to draft in extra engineering help from Peugeot to make it possible.

Porsche put a lot of work into making the roof of the 991-shape 911 cabriolet follow the line of the engine cover when seen in profile, as it does on the coupe. Designers disparagingly refer to the appearance of 996- and 997-shape cabrios, in which the profile of the car dips where roof meets metalwork and the ribs of the roof structure are visible through the fabric as "the hungry horse look".

*

Jaguar stopped building cars at its old Browns Lane factory in 2005 and most of the site was sold for re-development. But right up until the new Defender, all Jaguar Land Rover prototypes were still made there, in the old pilot build facility in one corner of the site. It's now moved to another part of Coventry.

*

BMC began using Farina to style its cars after an official visit to Longbridge by the Duke of Edinburgh in 1955 during which the famously outspoken royal told management that the in-house designs for future models he'd been shown were not up to the standards of foreign competition.

*

During development of the original Mini, BMC management showed the car to favoured design consultant Battista "Pinin" Farina and asked him for ways to improve it. "Leave it," the Italian maestro replied. "It is unique".

*

When the 'bug-eye' second generation Subaru Impreza WRX was facelifted it was due to get a smaller and more attractive bonnet scoop designed, like the rest of the update, in the UK by Peter Stevens. Unfortunately, in the wake of 9/11 Subaru executives were banned from flying and couldn't make it to Britain to sign off the new design so went with the existing, lumpen intake for the updated car, much to Stevens's chagrin.

*

MG Rover's first attempt at re-bodying the Qvale Mangusta was shown at the 2001 Frankfurt Motor Show as the X80 concept. The car on display during press day was a full-size clay model which reacted badly to the heat from the show stand lights and started to split apart at the base of the windscreen. The solution was to ask the two women booked to pose with the car to stand in front of the offending area at all times.

*

The famous wing on the back of the Lamborghini Countach was never homologated for sale. To get around this, any car ordered with it was wheeled out of the factory and into a car park where the wing could be fitted by a man with a drill, thereby meaning it was technically an aftermarket part rather than factory fitted.

*

The 1968 Ford Capri was signed off for production with a narrow rear side window with a reverse rake trailing edge, a bit like an AMC Gremlin, until engineers belatedly spent time in the back of a prototype and realised it felt claustrophobic. The designers' quick fix for the problem, just weeks before production was due to start, was the larger, D-shaped side window which became one of the car's signature features.

*

Until 2004 Peugeot created full-size styling models in polystyrene and plaster rather than the more common clay, not because this was like the traditional methods used by the great Italian styling houses but because models made of clay can weigh 2½ tonnes and the rooftop viewing area of their La Garenne-Colombes R&D centre couldn't take the weight. When Peugeot moved to a new, purpose-built design centre in Velizy they could start modelling in clay without fear of the floor collapsing.

*

The outside viewing area at Vauxhall's Luton design studio was highly secure until a block of flats was built nearby, the top of which was easily within telephoto lens range of the secret designs wheeled out of the studio. To solve the problem Vauxhall bought all the new flats with line of sight to their property and left them unoccupied. A few years later when the Luton studio was closed they were able to sell these flats for a tidy profit.

*

The Morris Ital wasn't designed by Giorgetto Giugiaro and Ital Design. The styling was by Harris Mann and his team at Longbridge. Ital just did the production engineering on the revised bodyshell because BL people were busy with the Metro. BL boss Michael Edwardes suggested cutting the proposed name, Marina Ital, to Ital alone in order to leverage the Italian connection, on the basis that there was no harm in letting people assume the car was styled in Turin and not Birmingham.

*

Some years ago, Jaguar had a clear out at its pilot build plant on Browns Lane in Coventry and found two unused XJ220 bodyshells under a load of cardboard boxes.

Paint colours offered on the short-lived, Aussie-only Leyland P76 saloon of the mid-seventies included;

- Am Eye Blue
- Bold As Brass
- Dry Red
- Hairy Lime
- Home On Th'Orange
- N.V. Green
- Peel Me A Grape
- Oh Fudge

Rostyle wheels are so-called because they were a style of wheel made by Rubery Owen. Hence, R. O. style.

*

The Renault Espace was conceived at Chrysler UK and given to Matra, who Chrysler owned at the time, to develop for Talbot. After Chrysler Europe was sold to Peugeot, the idea was binned, Matra became independent and successfully pitched the Espace concept to Renault. That's why the original Espace has forward raked headlights; when the car was first designed they were supposed to be carryover items from the Chrysler Alpine.

*

The man who designed the E28-shape BMW 5-series and the NSU Ro80 later went to prison for fatally stabbing his son. On Good Friday 1990 Claus Luthe got into an argument with his 33-year-old son, Ulrich, which culminated in the designer stabbing him to death. He was sentenced to 33 months in prison for manslaughter.

*

After the series 3 Allegro of 1979, BL planned an Allegro 4 with two-tone paint and other 'improvements' before realising they were pushing their luck and deciding to let the car run out its time as it was.

*

Art Blakeslee, one of the designers of the original Renault Espace, told his team during development that it was their 'silk shorts' car, meaning that it would be such a smash hit they'd all able to afford fancy undercrackers. In its first month on sale in France, Renault managed to sell just nine Espaces.

The designers of the original Ford Ka wanted each shape and surface to be so distinctive that you could see any panel from the car in isolation and know immediately where it was from.

*

When Jaguar was taken over by Ford in 1990 it was working on a brand-new big saloon, codenamed XJ90. When Bill Hayden, the Ford man installed as Jag CEO, was shown the clay model for the first time he liked it so much he declared that he was about to have an orgasm. Unfortunately for him, Ford wouldn't pay for an all new car to be developed so XJ90 design themes were adapted around the old XJ40 centre section to make the heavily revised X300 XJ of 1994.

*

The designers of the Ford Sierra were 'inspired' by the Porsche 928, as can be seen in the sculpting of the front wings and the shapes of the side windows. It's especially noticeable on the three-door XR4i. When lesser three-door Sierras came along, they had a single rear side window rather than the XR4i's weird two window arrangement because management felt the latter looked unbalanced without the sporty model's double decker rear spoiler.

*

The Talbot Tagora's rear axle always looked too narrow for its body because during development Chrysler Europe was bought by PSA (for the sum of one dollar) and the new bosses insisted the car should share parts with other models, landing it with a Peugeot 505 rear axle that wasn't quite wide enough.

After burning the midnight oil to get a clay model of their new Mini proposal ready for a management review the next day, designer Frank Stephenson's team celebrated finishing their work by cracking a few beers in the design studio. Then someone realised they'd forgotten to add an exhaust finisher to their model. With time running out, one of the designers stripped his Budweiser can to bare silver, punched a hole in the top and stuck it to the model. Management approved the car, including the improvised bit of trim, and the first BMW Mini Cooper went into production with an exhaust that looked like a beer can.

*

While other Group B rally cars resembled road-going hatchbacks and coupés from their makers' ranges, the Ford RS200 looked like no Ford on earth because the company sold different-looking cars in different parts of the world and didn't want to peg its new rally car to a specific model from any one region. The car's unique look was created (using Sierra parts including windscreen, tail lamps and cut-down doors) by a team that included future Jag design boss, Ian Callum.

*

The Fiat Coupé design team wanted to leave the car's distinctive fuel filler cap in bare chrome so that it would 'weather in' with an attractive patina. The warranty department disagreed and the fuel filler cap got a layer of protective lacquer for production. Although as Coupés get older this lacquer starts to peel off anyway.

*

In 1967 Volkswagen hired Pininfarina to design its new large car, a project that would eventually become the Passat. However, two years later bosses in Wolfsburg asked their Italian importer to walk around the Turin Motor Show and compile a list of the six best looking cars on display. When he sent through his findings, four of the six (De Tomaso Mangusta, Iso Rivolta, Iso Grifo, Maserati Ghibli) were the work of a young designer who had just started up his own design agency, Ital Design. On that basis, VW immediately contacted this designer and commissioned him to create a new car range to a consistent family look, binning off Pininfarina in the process. Which is how a young Giorgetto Giugiaro ended up designing the first Golf (and the original Passat and Scirocco).

\*

The Porsche 997 GT3 RS interior featured a lot of Alcantara because GT department boss Andreas Preuninger had developed a fondness for the stuff after owning several Lancia Delta Integrales.

# MEDIA

In 2001 Autocar scored quite a coup when they ran a spy picture of the forthcoming Rover 45 replacement but the lone photo of a heavily camouflaged prototype was not what it seemed. This wasn't long after BMW had sold Rover to the Phoenix Four for a symbolic ten quid and the newly-independent company was keen to show the world that it was working on new products. Unfortunately, at this point the Rover 45 replacement, codenamed RDX60, didn't actually exist in prototype form. So Rover's cunning PR team went down to their local B&Q, bought a shedload of bin bags and black tape, and set about 'camouflaging' an ordinary blue Rover 75. Then they took it down to the MIRA test track, snapped a long lens photo of it and crudely Photoshopped off the saloon boot so it looked like a bobtailed hatchback under the disguise. For the final part of their plan, a Rover PR took the editor of Autocar out for lunch and clumsily let the 'spy' photo 'accidentally' fall out of his bag. Autocar got a good cover story and Rover were able to give the impression that everything was going swimmingly under new management. The RDX60 project never made it to the running prototype stage, beyond a few mules that looked like normal Rover 75s.

\*

In the early seventies a journalist and photographer from a car magazine were left unattended inside Jaguar's Browns Lane factory and wandered into a room full of cars under dust sheets. The snapper pulled back the sheet from one unfamiliar-looking model and asked his colleague if he should take some pics. "Nah," said the journo. "Jag would never make something that ugly". A few years later the car went on sale as the XJ-S.

The very first edition of Auto Express, published in September 1988, carried a massive spy picture of the forthcoming second-generation Rover 200 on its cover under the headline, 'SECRET ROVER'. Since photo manipulation software was in its infancy back then, the camouflage was stripped off the prototype in the cover photo using Tippex.

*

Ill-fated nineties soap Eldorado reached its climax when loveable baddy Marcus Tandy got blown up in his Alpine A610. Closer inspection of the footage revealed that the A610 – then a new car worth almost £30,000 or about the same as a contemporary Range Rover Vogue – had been switched at the last moment for an old Triumph TR7, crudely doctored to look like the Alpine from head-on.

*

When Audi made a high-budget TV spot for the 2010 Superbowl featuring visions of a dystopian future patrolled by an environmental 'green police' no one at the ad agency realised that the title they used in the advert, *Ordnungspolizei,* was also the name of the 'order police' in Nazi Germany.

*

At the climax of the 2012 Bond film Skyfall, 007's Aston Martin DB5 is brutally machine gunned by a helicopter. Of course, it was too expensive to shoot up a real DB5 so the effect was achieved using a blend of CGI and scale models, but the film makers still needed a full-size object they could blast with special effects gunfire to provide a datum point for the post production work. The car they used for this role was a silver Porsche 928.

The October 1985 edition of CAR magazine carried brazen close-up scoop photos of the vital Austin Rover executive car that would be launched the following year as the Rover 800. The photos depicted a row of undisguised prototypes, apparently inside an ARG facility and, weirdly, flecked with water. To achieve this coup someone had set off the fire alarm and sprinklers within the building, causing an evacuation which gave the sneak plenty of time to photograph the top-secret pre-production cars before selling the pics to the highest bidder for a chunky sum of money.

*

In 1995 American spy photographer Jim Dunne bought a tract of desert land that poked straight into Chrysler's proving ground in Wittmann, Arizona. Thereafter, Dunne could legally snap the cars on their track and there wasn't much they could do to stop him.

*

The Aston DBS flip in Casino Royale was meant to be achieved with ramps alone, and was worked out at Dunsfold Aerodrome, home of Top Gear, using a pair of old E34 BMWs. Unfortunately, when the stunt people got hold of an actual Aston, the original DB9 manual gearbox prototype that was due for crushing, and took it to the filming location at Millbrook test track in Bedfordshire to practise, they found the centre of gravity too low to make the car roll, even when the ramp was raised to 18 inches, up from the originally calculated eight inches. The solution was to fit one of the three DBS stunt cars, actually dressed-up DB9 development hacks, with an air ram that punched into the road and flipped the car for the shot.

Before its official reveal in 1995 the MG F was one of the hottest topics for British car magazines yet not one of them had managed to snag any clear spy shots of a prototype on test. Determined to be first to this scoop, the editor of Autocar hired a helicopter and mounted an audacious raid on Rover's Gaydon proving ground, coming in low over the fields with a photographer hanging out of the side. Unfortunately, there were no MG F prototypes on the track at the time and they were unable to hang around since a) it was rather obvious what they were up to and b) the editor hadn't booked the chopper for very long because it was so expensive. The Autocar team flew away without sight of any MG Fs and just a few shots of the forthcoming but far less exciting Rover 400.

In 1992 James May was 'let go' from his job as production editor at Autocar & Motor after putting a hidden message in their road test yearbook compendium. The message, which was spelt out in the drop caps that started each road test, read as follows;

ROAD TEST YEAR BOOK SO YOU THINK IT S REALLY GOOD YEAH YOU SHOULD TRY MAKING THE BLOODY THING UP IT S A REAL PAIN IN THE ARSE.

May would have got away with it if readers hadn't started contacting the magazine assuming this was a competition and that by spotting the message they'd won some kind of prize.

Every lane on every high-speed bowl has a 'zero steer' speed at which the driver can take their hands off the wheel and the car will keep tracking on the correct line. The zero steer speed for the top lane of the bowl at the Millbrook test track in Bedfordshire is 100mph. In the nineties, Autocar writers Colin Goodwin and Steve Sutcliffe decided to test this by getting a Bentley Continental T up to 100, setting the cruise control, and then both climbing into the back seat. This was all extremely hilarious until, without warning, the Bentley's cruise control switched off. After an undignified scramble as they both tried to get back into the front at the same time, Goodwin and Sutcliffe miraculously re-gained control without binning the car.

*

In its January 1994 issue CAR magazine ran a scoop story on the forthcoming Jaguar XK8 and X300 XJ accurately revealing the cars' design, inside and out. Jag people immediately realised the shots had been taken inside their design studio and forensically analysed the pics until they spotted a reflection in a chrome gear knob from which they were able to identify the traitor.

*

Top Gear started in 1977 as a monthly half-hour programme shown only in the Midlands.

# PARTS SHARING

The upper shell of the ill-fated Sinclair C5 was made from the same ICI polypropylene compound as the bumpers on up-spec Austin Maestros.

*

The carbon fibre strips above each headlight on the 1998 Lamborghini Diablo facelift weren't merely cosmetic. They were also there to hide the prominent Nissan logo on the upper edge of each unit because the lamps were taken from the 300ZX.

*

The Range Rover Velar features a modern, minimalist interior, but the optional rear seat recline function is operated by a generic Ford switch of a style first seen in the 1985 'aero' Granada.

*

All but early Lamborghini Countachs used Lucas-made column stalks, first seen in the Morris Marina. Rather than buy right-hand-drive stalks, back when RHD cars had the indicator stalk on the right, Lamborghini simply rotated the entire left-hand-drive column stalks assembly through 180 degrees. This made the symbols on the stalks upsidedown, a problem they corrected with the application of little stickers.

*

The 1996 Jaguar XKR and 1997 XJR used a Mercedes gearbox rather than the ZF unit of lesser models.

*

The Pagani Zonda and the late model Rover 45 use the same climate control panel. It's a generic, off-the-shelf unit made by an Italian company called Bitron and also found, hidden under a flap, in the Lamborghini Murcielago.

91

The 1989 Lotus Elan was supposed to use Isuzu Piazza rear lights, hidden under a smoked cover. Late in development Lotus went to check these lights for compliance and found they weren't bright enough to be legal, even with the smoked covers taken off. At the last minute they were replaced with units from the Renault Alpine GTA which fitted into the holes in the Elan's body without much adjustment. As an added bonus, when Lotus contacted Renault about using this lamp they discovered there was a US-spec version on the shelf as a hangover from an abandoned plan to sell the GTA in North America. The idea to use the Renault lamps came to Elan designer Peter Stevens one Sunday evening while watching eighties yacht schlock drama Howard's Way in which one of the characters drove a GTA.

The Aston Martin DB7 was developed on a shoestring budget of $30 million, barely what many car makers would spend on a light facelift. This meant using various bits from the wider Ford parts bin including Mazda 323F rear lights, mk1 MX5 interior door handles and generic Ford switches (plus the entire understructure from the Jaguar XJ-S). This gave designer Ian Callum a problem when picking exterior door handles because Aston boss Walter Hayes insisted they must have a chrome finish and, since such things weren't very fashionable in the nineties, the design team couldn't find a single contemporary Ford that featured something suitable. That is until they discovered the one model in the entire empire that still used chrome handles. And this is why the DB7 has the exterior door handles from an up-spec, Japanese-market version of the Mazda 323 estate.

## CARS THAT USED THE
## CITROËN CX SERIES 2 DOOR MIRROR

AC Ace
Aixam MEGA Track
Aston Martin DB7
Aston Martin Vantage
Aston Martin Virage
Citroën CX series 2
Jaguar XJ220
Lotus Esprit
Lotus Excel
Marcos Mantis/Mantara/Mantaray/Marcasite
Renault Sport Spider
TVR Chimera
TVR Griffith
TVR S3/S4
Venturi Atlantique

In 1985 Citroën facelifted the CX, giving it what it described at the time as "new aerodynamic door mirrors". These mirrors would become the go-to for many exotic-ish cars for years to come. A set even fetched up on the third prototype of the McLaren F1, though production F1s switched to using Volkswagen Corrado mirrors. One reason the CX series 2 mirror became so popular on low volume cars is that it looked modern yet still mounted to the door skin itself like an old-fashioned side mirror, rather than needing a bespoke mount to attach to the corner of the door glass, as became the trend in the eighties and nineties. Aston DB7 designer Ian Callum shed some more light on the appeal of the CX mirror when he said, "They were the only mirrors that looked really cool we could afford".

When the Austin Montego debuted in 1984 it introduced a neat new electric mirror adjuster that was then used across many cars from Austin Rover and its successors including the Austin Maestro, Land Rover Discovery, Range Rover Classic, Rover 200 and 25 and the MG F and TF. Lucas, who made the switch, must have had a good sales rep in Italy because the same mirror control was also used in the Ferrari Testarossa and the Maserati Biturbo and Ghibli II. These, however, are not the most surprising cars to use the switch since it also appeared in the Jaguar XJR- endurance racing cars which, surprisingly, had electric mirrors to make it easy for drivers to adjust them after taking over from a team mate mid-race. The last new car to use the Montego mirror adjuster was the MG TF which finally went out of production in 2011.

*

Prototypes of the 2001 Aston Martin Vanquish used Ford Ka dashboard vents and rear lights from the Ford Cougar (but masked and with covers to hide their origins). When Ulrich Bez joined the company in 2000 his objection to these parts led him to sign off the money for more expensive Volvo dash vents and bespoke tail lamps.

*

The McLaren F1 used off-the-shelf rear lights made by Cobo of Italy and also seen on the Lamborghini Diablo and the Bova Futura coach.

*

When Aston Martin, Jaguar, Land Rover, Lincoln and Volvo were lumped together as Premier Automotive Group under Ford ownership, Volvo was tasked with developing a new electrical architecture which could be used across the group. The job wasn't completed before the different manufacturers started doing their own things and PAG began to splinter, but you can see a tiny legacy of it in the Volvo-style electric mirror adjuster still used in many Jags to this day.

*

Rear lights used by the Lotus Esprit:
- Series 1 – Fiat X1/9
- Series 2 and 3 – Rover SD1
- '87 facelift – Toyota Corolla Levin AE86
- '02 update – Lotus Elise series 2

# CARS THAT USED THE MARINA FLAP

Africar
Austin Allegro
Elswick Envoy
Ginetta G15 (late models)
Ginetta G21
Land Rover Discovery mk1
Lotus Eclat
Lotus Elite
Lotus Esprit
Morris Marina
Range Rover mk1 five door
Reliant Scimitar GTE SE6
Trident Clipper/Ventura (late models)
Triumph TR7/TR8

With the 1971 Morris Marina, British Leyland debuted a new, flap-style exterior door handle that was subsequently used on many other cars. The design of the flap seems to have been inspired by a similar device introduced by AMC across most of its cars in 1968. The last series production car to use the Marina flap was the Land Rover Discovery which was made until 1998.

Not all Marina flaps are the same, however. The ones introduced on the TR7 and later used on the five-door Range Rover are a slightly different design and supposedly of higher quality.

# THANKS TO

Alex Fisk, Alex Goy, Angus Fitton, Ash Sutcliffe, Colin Goodwin, David Inglis, David Pook, Ian Seabrook, James May, Jeremy Townsend, Keith Adams, Kyle Fortune, Lance Bradley, Lee Walton, Michael Harvey, Paul Horrell, Richard Aucock, Rob Halloway, Simon Charlesworth, Tom Barnard, @frogginbullfish.

Special thanks to Keith WR Jones

# REFERENCE MATERIAL

Here are just some of the sources of information used in compiling this book.

45 Years Without John DeLorean by Barrie Wills
AROnline
Autocar
Back From The Brink by Michael Edwardes
CAR
Car Guys vs Bean Counters: The Battle For The Soul Of American Business by Bob Lutz
Car Spy by Jim Dunne
Citroënet
End of the Road: BMW and Rover: A Brand Too Far by Chris Brady and Andrew Lorenz
evo
Ford Cortina: The Complete History by Russell Hayes
Let's Call It Fiesta by Edouard Seidler
Lotus Elan by Mark Hughes
Metro: The Book of the Car by Graham Robson
Rally Group B Shrine
Range Rover Second Generation: The Complete Story by James Taylor
The Road Rat